Finance Planner

I. S. Anderson

Finance Planner

Copyright © 2022 by I. S. Anderson

ISBN-10: 1-947399-38-1

ISBN-13: 978-1-947399-38-9

All rights reserved, including the right to reproduce this journal in whole or any portions thereof, in any form whatsoever.

For more information regarding this publication, contact: **nahjpress@outlook.com**

First Printing, 2022

Finance Planner

Belongs To:

_____

Sample Page

Income and Fixed Expenses

Month: *March*   Year: *2022*

Date	Source of Income	Amount
01/14	Salary	3,500.00
01/16	Rental income	1,800.00
01/21	Writing	900.00
01/28	Salary	3,500.00
	Total Income	9,700.00

Savings	Amount
Emergency fund	1,0000.00
Investments	2,000.00
Vacation	1,0000.00
Total Savings	4,000.00

Due Date	Fixed Expenses	Amount
01/02	Mortgage	2,200.00
01/07	Car insurance	150.00
01/10	Car payment	500.00
01/15	Internet	60.00
01/15	Subscriptions	40.00
	Total Fixed Expenses	2,950

Credit Card	Payment	Balance
Visa	300.00	0
	Total 300.00	0

Total Income		9,700.00
-	Total Fixed Expenses	2,950.00
-	Total Credit Card Payment	300.00
-	Total Savings	4000.00
Remaining Balance		2,450.00

Sample Page

Weekly/Monthly Budget

Expense	Budgeted	Actual
Electricity	120.00	134.00
Water	70.00	70.00
Gas	170.00	165.00
Grocery	400.00	455.00
Personal care	200.00	150.00
Subtotal	960.00	974.00

Expense	Budgeted	Actual
Subtotal		

	Budgeted	Actual
Subtotal		

	Budgeted	Actual
Subtotal		

Summary	Amount
Previous Balance	2,450.00
− Total Actual Expenses	974.00
Remaining Balance	1,476.00

My Financial Goals

Goal:	Time Frame:
	Notes:

Goal:	Time Frame:
	Notes:

Goal:	Time Frame:
	Notes:

Goal:	Time Frame:
	Notes:

My Financial Goals

Goal:	Time Frame:
	Notes:

Goal:	Time Frame:
	Notes:

Goal:	Time Frame:
	Notes:

Goal:	Time Frame:
	Notes:

My Net Worth

Assets (What I Own)

Cash and Cash Equivalents	Amount
Checking account	
Savings account	
Money market account	
Cash value of life insurance	
Total	

Real Estate	Current Value
Principal home	
Vacation home	
Land	
Total	

Investments	Current Value
Certificates of deposit	
Stocks	
Bonds	
Mutual funds	
Annuity (accumulated value)	
IRAs	
401(k)/ 403(b) /457 plans	
Pension plan	
Total	

Personal Property	Current Value
Cars, trucks, boats	
Home furnishings	
Art, antiques, coins, collectibles	
Jewelry	
Total	
Total Assets	

Liabilities (What I Owe)

Current Debts	Amount Due
Credit card balances	
Estimated income tax owed	
Medical	
Legal	
Total	

Long-term Debts	Amount Due
Home mortgage	
Home equity loan	
Mortgage on rental properties	
Car loans	
Student loans	
Life insurance policy loans	
Total	
Total Liabilities	

Net Worth	
(Total Assets – Total Liabilities)	

Notes

My Net Worth

Assets (What I Own)

Cash and Cash Equivalents	Amount
Checking account	
Savings account	
Money market account	
Cash value of life insurance	
Total	

Real Estate	Current Value
Principal home	
Vacation home	
Land	
Total	

Investments	Current Value
Certificates of deposit	
Stocks	
Bonds	
Mutual funds	
Annuity (accumulated value)	
IRAs	
401(k)/ 403(b) /457 plans	
Pension plan	
Total	

Personal Property	Current Value
Cars, trucks, boats	
Home furnishings	
Art, antiques, coins, collectibles	
Jewelry	
Total	
Total Assets	

Liabilities (What I Owe)

Current Debts	Amount Due
Credit card balances	
Estimated income tax owed	
Medical	
Legal	
Total	

Long-term Debts	Amount Due
Home mortgage	
Home equity loan	
Mortgage on rental properties	
Car loans	
Student loans	
Life insurance policy loans	
Total	
Total Liabilities	

Net Worth	
(Total Assets – Total Liabilities)	

Notes

Month & Year: _____

SUNDAY	MONDAY	TUESDAY	WEDNESDAY

THURSDAY	FRIDAY	SATURDAY	NOTES
☐	☐	☐	
☐	☐	☐	
☐	☐	☐	
☐	☐	☐	
☐	☐	☐	

Income and Fixed Expenses

Month: _____   Year: _____

Date	Source of Income	Amount
	Total Income	

Savings	Amount
Total Savings	

Due Date	Fixed Expenses	Amount
	Total Fixed Expenses	

Credit Card	Payment	Balance
	Total	

Total Income	
- Total Fixed Expenses	
- Total Credit Card Payment	
- Total Savings	
Remaining Balance	

Weekly/Monthly Budget

Expense	Budgeted	Actual
Subtotal		

Expense	Budgeted	Actual
Subtotal		

Expense	Budgeted	Actual
Subtotal		

Expense	Budgeted	Actual
Subtotal		

Summary	Amount
Previous Balance	
− Total Actual Expenses	
Remaining Balance	

Daily Expenses

Date	Description/Category	Amount		Date	Description/Category	Amount
	Total				Total	

Daily Expenses

Date	Description/Category	Amount	Date	Description/Category	Amount
	Total			Total	

Ideas and Notes

Month: _____

Month & Year: _____

SUNDAY	MONDAY	TUESDAY	WEDNESDAY

THURSDAY	FRIDAY	SATURDAY	NOTES
☐	☐	☐	
☐	☐	☐	
☐	☐	☐	
☐	☐	☐	
☐	☐	☐	
☐	☐	☐	
☐	☐	☐	
☐	☐	☐	
☐	☐	☐	
☐	☐	☐	

Income and Fixed Expenses

Month: _____   Year: _____

Date	Source of Income	Amount
	Total Income	

Savings	Amount
Total Savings	

Due Date	Fixed Expenses	Amount
	Total Fixed Expenses	

Credit Card	Payment	Balance
	Total	

Total Income	
- Total Fixed Expenses	
- Total Credit Card Payment	
- Total Savings	
Remaining Balance	

Weekly/Monthly Budget

Expense	Budgeted	Actual
Subtotal		

Expense	Budgeted	Actual
Subtotal		

Subtotal		

Subtotal		

Summary	Amount
Previous Balance	
− Total Actual Expenses	
Remaining Balance	

Daily Expenses

Date	Description/Category	Amount	Date	Description/Category	Amount
	Total			Total	

Daily Expenses

Date	Description/Category	Amount	Date	Description/Category	Amount
	Total			Total	

Ideas and Notes

Month: _____

Month & Year: _____

SUNDAY	MONDAY	TUESDAY	WEDNESDAY

THURSDAY	FRIDAY	SATURDAY	NOTES
☐	☐	☐	
☐	☐	☐	
☐	☐	☐	
☐	☐	☐	
☐	☐	☐	
☐	☐	☐	
☐	☐	☐	
☐	☐	☐	
☐	☐	☐	
☐	☐	☐	
THURSDAY	FRIDAY	SATURDAY	NOTES

Income and Fixed Expenses

Month: _____   Year: _____

Date	Source of Income	Amount
	Total Income	

Savings	Amount
Total Savings	

Due Date	Fixed Expenses	Amount
	Total Fixed Expenses	

Credit Card	Payment	Balance
	Total	

Total Income	
- Total Fixed Expenses	
- Total Credit Card Payment	
- Total Savings	
Remaining Balance	

Weekly/Monthly Budget

Expense	Budgeted	Actual
Subtotal		

Expense	Budgeted	Actual
Subtotal		

Subtotal		

Subtotal		

Summary	Amount
Previous Balance	
- Total Actual Expenses	
Remaining Balance	

Daily Expenses

Date	Description/Category	Amount	Date	Description/Category	Amount
		Total			Total

Daily Expenses

Date	Description/Category	Amount		Date	Description/Category	Amount
		Total				Total

Ideas and Notes

Month: _____

Month & Year: _____

SUNDAY	MONDAY	TUESDAY	WEDNESDAY

| SUNDAY | MONDAY | TUESDAY | WEDNESDAY |

THURSDAY	FRIDAY	SATURDAY	NOTES
☐	☐	☐	
☐	☐	☐	
☐	☐	☐	
☐	☐	☐	
☐	☐	☐	

Income and Fixed Expenses

Month: _____   Year: _____

Date	Source of Income	Amount
	Total Income	

Savings		Amount
Total Savings		

Due Date	Fixed Expenses	Amount
	Total Fixed Expenses	

Credit Card	Payment	Balance
	Total	

	Total Income	
-	Total Fixed Expenses	
-	Total Credit Card Payment	
-	Total Savings	
	Remaining Balance	

Weekly/Monthly Budget

Expense	Budgeted	Actual
Subtotal		

Expense	Budgeted	Actual
Subtotal		

Subtotal		

Subtotal		

Summary	Amount
Previous Balance	
- Total Actual Expenses	
Remaining Balance	

Daily Expenses

Date	Description/Category	Amount	Date	Description/Category	Amount
		Total			Total

Daily Expenses

Date	Description/Category	Amount		Date	Description/Category	Amount
		Total				Total

Ideas and Notes

Month: _____

Month & Year: _____

SUNDAY	MONDAY	TUESDAY	WEDNESDAY

SUNDAY	MONDAY	TUESDAY	WEDNESDAY

THURSDAY	FRIDAY	SATURDAY	NOTES
☐	☐	☐	
☐	☐	☐	
☐	☐	☐	
☐	☐	☐	
☐	☐	☐	
☐	☐	☐	
☐	☐	☐	
☐	☐	☐	
☐	☐	☐	

Income and Fixed Expenses

Month: _____   Year: _____

Date	Source of Income	Amount
	Total Income	

Savings	Amount
Total Savings	

Due Date	Fixed Expenses	Amount
	Total Fixed Expenses	

Credit Card	Payment	Balance
	Total	

Total Income	
- Total Fixed Expenses	
- Total Credit Card Payment	
- Total Savings	
Remaining Balance	

Weekly/Monthly Budget

Expense	Budgeted	Actual
Subtotal		

Expense	Budgeted	Actual
Subtotal		

Subtotal		

Subtotal		

Summary	Amount
Previous Balance	
− Total Actual Expenses	
Remaining Balance	

Daily Expenses

Date	Description/Category	Amount	Date	Description/Category	Amount
	Total			Total	

Daily Expenses

Date	Description/Category	Amount
	Total	

Date	Description/Category	Amount
	Total	

Ideas and Notes

Month: _____

Month & Year: _____

SUNDAY	MONDAY	TUESDAY	WEDNESDAY
☐	☐	☐	☐
☐	☐	☐	☐
☐	☐	☐	☐
☐	☐	☐	☐
☐	☐	☐	☐
☐	☐	☐	☐
SUNDAY	MONDAY	TUESDAY	WEDNESDAY

THURSDAY	FRIDAY	SATURDAY	NOTES
☐	☐	☐	
☐	☐	☐	
☐	☐	☐	
☐	☐	☐	
☐	☐	☐	

Income and Fixed Expenses

Month: _____   Year: _____

Date	Source of Income	Amount
	Total Income	

Savings	Amount
Total Savings	

Due Date	Fixed Expenses	Amount
	Total Fixed Expenses	

Credit Card	Payment	Balance
	Total	

Total Income	
- Total Fixed Expenses	
- Total Credit Card Payment	
- Total Savings	
Remaining Balance	

Weekly/Monthly Budget

Expense	Budgeted	Actual
Subtotal		

Expense	Budgeted	Actual
Subtotal		

Subtotal		

Subtotal		

Summary	Amount
Previous Balance	
- Total Actual Expenses	
Remaining Balance	

Daily Expenses

Date	Description/Category	Amount	Date	Description/Category	Amount
		Total			Total

Daily Expenses

Date	Description/Category	Amount	Date	Description/Category	Amount
	Total			Total	

Ideas and Notes

Month: _____

Month & Year: _____

SUNDAY	MONDAY	TUESDAY	WEDNESDAY

| SUNDAY | MONDAY | TUESDAY | WEDNESDAY |

THURSDAY	FRIDAY	SATURDAY	NOTES
☐	☐	☐	
☐	☐	☐	
☐	☐	☐	
☐	☐	☐	
☐	☐	☐	
☐	☐	☐	
☐	☐	☐	
☐	☐	☐	
☐	☐	☐	

Income and Fixed Expenses

Month: _____   Year: _____

Date	Source of Income	Amount
	Total Income	

Savings	Amount
Total Savings	

Due Date	Fixed Expenses	Amount
	Total Fixed Expenses	

Credit Card	Payment	Balance
	Total	

Total Income	
- Total Fixed Expenses	
- Total Credit Card Payment	
- Total Savings	
Remaining Balance	

Weekly/Monthly Budget

Expense	Budgeted	Actual
Subtotal		

Expense	Budgeted	Actual
Subtotal		

Subtotal		

Subtotal		

Summary	Amount
Previous Balance	
- Total Actual Expenses	
Remaining Balance	

Daily Expenses

Date	Description/Category	Amount	Date	Description/Category	Amount
		Total			Total

Daily Expenses

Date	Description/Category	Amount		Date	Description/Category	Amount
		Total				Total

Ideas and Notes

Month: _____

Month & Year: _____

SUNDAY	MONDAY	TUESDAY	WEDNESDAY

SUNDAY	MONDAY	TUESDAY	WEDNESDAY

THURSDAY	FRIDAY	SATURDAY	NOTES
☐	☐	☐	
☐	☐	☐	
☐	☐	☐	
☐	☐	☐	
☐	☐	☐	
☐	☐	☐	
☐	☐	☐	
☐	☐	☐	
☐	☐	☐	

Income and Fixed Expenses

Month: _____   Year: _____

Date	Source of Income	Amount
	Total Income	

Savings	Amount
Total Savings	

Due Date	Fixed Expenses	Amount
	Total Fixed Expenses	

Credit Card	Payment	Balance
Total		

Total Income	
− Total Fixed Expenses	
− Total Credit Card Payment	
− Total Savings	
Remaining Balance	

Weekly/Monthly Budget

Expense	Budgeted	Actual
Subtotal		

Expense	Budgeted	Actual
Subtotal		

Subtotal		

Subtotal		

Summary	Amount
Previous Balance	
- Total Actual Expenses	
Remaining Balance	

Daily Expenses

Date	Description/Category	Amount	Date	Description/Category	Amount
	Total			Total	

Daily Expenses

Date	Description/Category	Amount	Date	Description/Category	Amount
		Total			Total

Ideas and Notes

Month: _____

Month & Year: _____

SUNDAY	MONDAY	TUESDAY	WEDNESDAY

SUNDAY   MONDAY   TUESDAY   WEDNESDAY

THURSDAY	FRIDAY	SATURDAY	NOTES
☐	☐	☐	
☐	☐	☐	
☐	☐	☐	
☐	☐	☐	
☐	☐	☐	

Income and Fixed Expenses

Month: _____   Year: _____

Date	Source of Income	Amount
	Total Income	

Savings	Amount
Total Savings	

Due Date	Fixed Expenses	Amount
	Total Fixed Expenses	

Credit Card	Payment	Balance
Total		

	Total Income	
-	Total Fixed Expenses	
-	Total Credit Card Payment	
-	Total Savings	
	Remaining Balance	

Weekly/Monthly Budget

Expense	Budgeted	Actual
Subtotal		

Expense	Budgeted	Actual
Subtotal		

Subtotal		

Subtotal		

Summary	Amount
Previous Balance	
- Total Actual Expenses	
Remaining Balance	

Daily Expenses

Date	Description/Category	Amount
	Total	

Date	Description/Category	Amount
	Total	

Daily Expenses

Date	Description/Category	Amount
	Total	

Date	Description/Category	Amount
	Total	

Ideas and Notes

Month: _____

Month & Year: _____

SUNDAY	MONDAY	TUESDAY	WEDNESDAY

Month & Year: _____

SUNDAY	MONDAY	TUESDAY	WEDNESDAY

THURSDAY	FRIDAY	SATURDAY	NOTES
☐	☐	☐	
☐	☐	☐	
☐	☐	☐	
☐	☐	☐	
☐	☐	☐	

Income and Fixed Expenses

Month: _____   Year: _____

Date	Source of Income	Amount
	Total Income	

Savings	Amount
Total Savings	

Due Date	Fixed Expenses	Amount
	Total Fixed Expenses	

Credit Card	Payment	Balance
	Total	

Total Income	
- Total Fixed Expenses	
- Total Credit Card Payment	
- Total Savings	
Remaining Balance	

Weekly/Monthly Budget

Expense	Budgeted	Actual
Subtotal		

Expense	Budgeted	Actual
Subtotal		

Subtotal		

Subtotal		

Summary	Amount
Previous Balance	
- Total Actual Expenses	
Remaining Balance	

Daily Expenses

Date	Description/Category	Amount	Date	Description/Category	Amount
	Total			Total	

Daily Expenses

Date	Description/Category	Amount	Date	Description/Category	Amount
		Total			Total

Ideas and Notes

Month: _____

Month & Year: _____

SUNDAY	MONDAY	TUESDAY	WEDNESDAY

| SUNDAY | MONDAY | TUESDAY | WEDNESDAY |

THURSDAY	FRIDAY	SATURDAY	NOTES
☐	☐	☐	
☐	☐	☐	
☐	☐	☐	
☐	☐	☐	
☐	☐	☐	
☐	☐	☐	
☐	☐	☐	
☐	☐	☐	
☐	☐	☐	
☐	☐	☐	

Income and Fixed Expenses

Month: _____   Year: _____

Date	Source of Income	Amount
	Total Income	

Savings	Amount
Total Savings	

Due Date	Fixed Expenses	Amount
	Total Fixed Expenses	

Credit Card	Payment	Balance
	Total	

Total Income	
- Total Fixed Expenses	
- Total Credit Card Payment	
- Total Savings	
Remaining Balance	

Weekly/Monthly Budget

Expense	Budgeted	Actual
Subtotal		

Expense	Budgeted	Actual
Subtotal		

Subtotal		

Subtotal		

Summary	Amount
Previous Balance	
- Total Actual Expenses	
Remaining Balance	

Daily Expenses

Date	Description/Category	Amount	Date	Description/Category	Amount
	Total			Total	

Daily Expenses

Date	Description/Category	Amount	Date	Description/Category	Amount
	Total			Total	

Ideas and Notes

Month: _____

Month & Year: _____

SUNDAY	MONDAY	TUESDAY	WEDNESDAY

| SUNDAY | MONDAY | TUESDAY | WEDNESDAY |

THURSDAY	FRIDAY	SATURDAY	NOTES

Income and Fixed Expenses

Month: _____   Year: _____

Date	Source of Income	Amount
	Total Income	

Savings	Amount
Total Savings	

Due Date	Fixed Expenses	Amount
	Total Fixed Expenses	

Credit Card	Payment	Balance
	Total	

Total Income		
-	Total Fixed Expenses	
-	Total Credit Card Payment	
-	Total Savings	
Remaining Balance		

Weekly/Monthly Budget

Expense	Budgeted	Actual
Subtotal		

Expense	Budgeted	Actual
Subtotal		

Subtotal		

Subtotal		

Summary	Amount
Previous Balance	
- Total Actual Expenses	
Remaining Balance	

Daily Expenses

Date	Description/Category	Amount	Date	Description/Category	Amount
		Total			Total

Daily Expenses

Date	Description/Category	Amount
		Total

Date	Description/Category	Amount
		Total

Ideas and Notes

Savings, Debt, and Bill Trackers

Savings Tracker

Saving for	Amount Needed	Due Date

Date	Deposit	Balance

Saving for	Amount Needed	Due Date

Date	Deposit	Balance

Saving for	Amount Needed	Due Date

Date	Deposit	Balance

Saving for	Amount Needed	Due Date

Date	Deposit	Balance

Savings Tracker

Saving for	Amount Needed	Due Date

Date	Deposit	Balance

Saving for	Amount Needed	Due Date

Date	Deposit	Balance

Saving for	Amount Needed	Due Date

Date	Deposit	Balance

Saving for	Amount Needed	Due Date

Date	Deposit	Balance

Savings Tracker

Saving for	Amount Needed	Due Date

Date	Deposit	Balance

Saving for	Amount Needed	Due Date

Date	Deposit	Balance

Saving for	Amount Needed	Due Date

Date	Deposit	Balance

Saving for	Amount Needed	Due Date

Date	Deposit	Balance

Savings Tracker

Saving for	Amount Needed	Due Date

Date	Deposit	Balance

Saving for	Amount Needed	Due Date

Date	Deposit	Balance

Saving for	Amount Needed	Due Date

Date	Deposit	Balance

Saving for	Amount Needed	Due Date

Date	Deposit	Balance

Debt Tracker

Name of Creditor: _____

Date	Starting Balance	Interest Rate	Minimum Payment	Amount Paid	Ending Balance

Name of Creditor: _____

Date	Starting Balance	Interest Rate	Minimum Payment	Amount Paid	Ending Balance

Debt Tracker

Name of Creditor: _____

Date	Starting Balance	Interest Rate	Minimum Payment	Amount Paid	Ending Balance

Name of Creditor: _____

Date	Starting Balance	Interest Rate	Minimum Payment	Amount Paid	Ending Balance

Debt Tracker

Name of Creditor: _____

Date	Starting Balance	Interest Rate	Minimum Payment	Amount Paid	Ending Balance

Name of Creditor: _____

Date	Starting Balance	Interest Rate	Minimum Payment	Amount Paid	Ending Balance

Debt Tracker

Name of Creditor: _____

Date	Starting Balance	Interest Rate	Minimum Payment	Amount Paid	Ending Balance

Name of Creditor: _____

Date	Starting Balance	Interest Rate	Minimum Payment	Amount Paid	Ending Balance

Debt Tracker

Name of Creditor: _____

Date	Starting Balance	Interest Rate	Minimum Payment	Amount Paid	Ending Balance

Name of Creditor: _____

Date	Starting Balance	Interest Rate	Minimum Payment	Amount Paid	Ending Balance

Debt Tracker

Name of Creditor: _____

Date	Starting Balance	Interest Rate	Minimum Payment	Amount Paid	Ending Balance

Name of Creditor: _____

Date	Starting Balance	Interest Rate	Minimum Payment	Amount Paid	Ending Balance

Debt Tracker

Name of Creditor: _____

Date	Starting Balance	Interest Rate	Minimum Payment	Amount Paid	Ending Balance

Name of Creditor: _____

Date	Starting Balance	Interest Rate	Minimum Payment	Amount Paid	Ending Balance

Debt Tracker

Name of Creditor: _____

Date	Starting Balance	Interest Rate	Minimum Payment	Amount Paid	Ending Balance

Name of Creditor: _____

Date	Starting Balance	Interest Rate	Minimum Payment	Amount Paid	Ending Balance

Holiday Budget

Expense	Budgeted	Actual
Total		

Expense	Budgeted	Actual
Total		

Holiday Gifts

Recipient	Budgeted	Actual
Total		

Recipient	Budgeted	Actual
Total		

Holiday Spending

Date	Description/Category	Amount
	Total	

Date	Description/Category	Amount
	Total	

Bill Tracker

Bill Name \ Month						

Bill Tracker

Bill Name / Month						

Summary for the Year

Month						
Total Income						
Total Expenses						
Balance						
Total Savings						

Monthly Expenses Summary

Category/Expense						

Summary for the Year

Month						
Total Income						
Total Expenses						
Balance						
Total Savings						

Monthly Expenses Summary

Category/Expense						

Accounts Information

Name:	Account:
Website:	Username:
Password/Hint:	
Notes:	

Name:	Account:
Website:	Username:
Password/Hint:	
Notes:	

Name:	Account:
Website:	Username:
Password/Hint:	
Notes:	

Name:	Account:
Website:	Username:
Password/Hint:	
Notes:	

Name:	Account:
Website:	Username:
Password/Hint:	
Notes:	

Name:	Account:
Website:	Username:
Password/Hint:	
Notes:	

Name:	Account:
Website:	Username:
Password/Hint:	
Notes:	

Name:	Account:
Website:	Username:
Password/Hint:	
Notes:	

Accounts Information

Name:	Account:
Website:	Username:
Password/Hint:	
Notes:	

Name:	Account:
Website:	Username:
Password/Hint:	
Notes:	

Name:	Account:
Website:	Username:
Password/Hint:	
Notes:	

Name:	Account:
Website:	Username:
Password/Hint:	
Notes:	

Name:	Account:
Website:	Username:
Password/Hint:	
Notes:	

Name:	Account:
Website:	Username:
Password/Hint:	
Notes:	

Name:	Account:
Website:	Username:
Password/Hint:	
Notes:	

Name:	Account:
Website:	Username:
Password/Hint:	
Notes:	

www.ingramcontent.com/pod-product-compliance
Lightning Source LLC
Chambersburg PA
CBHW080458240426
43673CB00005B/233